best smooth jazz

Arranged by Brent Edstrom

T0071450

contents

ISBN 978-1-4950-9349-4

7777 W. BLUEMOUND RD. P.O. BOX 13819 MILWAUKEE, WI 53213

Visit Hal Leonard Online at
www.halleonard.com

AFTER HOURS
(The Antidote)

By RONALD LES ALBERT SIMPSON

Arrangement based on one by Ronny Jordan

ANTHEM FOR A NEW AMERICA

By JEFF LORBER
and BOBBY COLOMBY

Arrangement based on one by Jeff Lorber

BOSSA BAROQUE

By DAVE GRUSIN

Arrangement based on one by Dave Grusin

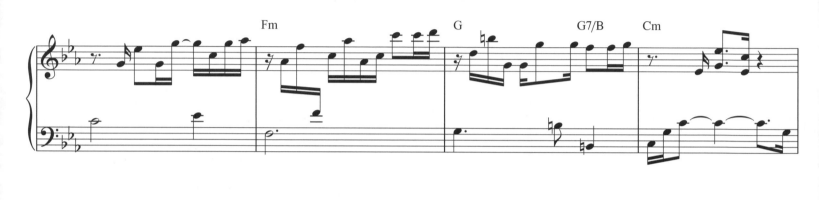

BREEZIN'

Words and Music by
BOBBY WOMACK

Moderately fast

Arrangement based on one by George Benson

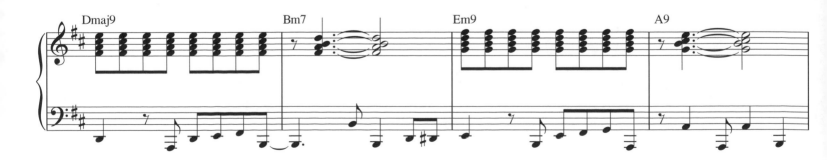

FEELS SO GOOD

By CHUCK MANGIONE

Arrangement based on one by Chuck Mangione

Solo based on a transcription by Grant Geissman

CAUSE WE'VE ENDED AS LOVERS

Words and Music by
STEVIE WONDER

Arrangement based on one by Chieli Minucci

FREEDOM EITHER WAY

By HARVEY MASON

Arrangement based on one by Dave Grusin

FOREVER IN LOVE

By KENNY G

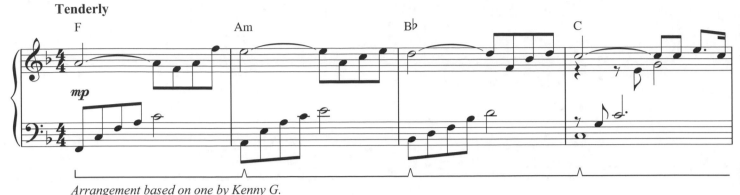

Arrangement based on one by Kenny G.

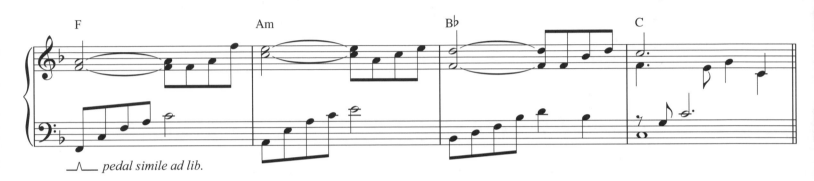

ISABELLA

By GREGORY KARUKAS

Arrangement based on one by Gregg Karukas

KEI'S SONG

By DAVID BENOIT

Arrangement based on one by David Benoit

PROTOTYPE

By JEFF LORBER

Arrangement based on one by Jeff Lorber

MAPUTO

By MARCUS MILLER

101 EASTBOUND

By MARCEL EAST
and NATHAN EAST

Moderately slow

Arrangement based on one by Fourplay

RISE

By RANDY BADAZZ
and ANDY ARMER

Medium funky groove

Arrangement based on one by Herb Alpert

SENSUALITY

By BRIAN CULBERTSON
and STEPHEN LU

Moderately slow

Arrangement based on one by Brian Culbertson

SHAKER SONG

By JAY BECKENSTEIN

Arrangement based on one by Spyro Gyra

SO AMAZING

Words and Music by
LUTHER VANDROSS

Slowly, with feeling

Arrangement based on one by Gerald Albright

SMILES AND SMILES TO GO

By LARRY CARLTON

Arrangement based on one by Larry Carlton

WHEN I SAY YOUR NAME

By DAVE KOZ
and BRIAN SIMPSON

Moderately slow Latin groove

Arrangement based on one by Brian Simpson

YOU MAKE ME SMILE

By DAVE KOZ
and JEFF KOZ

Arrangement based on one by Dave Koz

WISHFUL THINKING

Words and Music by
EARL KLUGH

Arrangement based on one by Earl Klugh

The Best-Selling Jazz Book of All Time Is Now Legal!

The Real Books are the most popular jazz books of all time. Since the 1970s, musicians have trusted these volumes to get them through every gig, night after night. The problem is that the books were illegally produced and distributed, without any regard to copyright law, or royalties paid to the composers who created these musical masterpieces.

Hal Leonard is very proud to present the first legitimate and legal editions of these books ever produced. You won't even notice the difference, other than all the notorious errors being fixed: the covers and typeface look the same, the song lists are nearly identical, and the price for our edition is even cheaper than the originals!

Every conscientious musician will appreciate that these books are now produced accurately and ethically, benefitting the songwriters that we owe for some of the greatest tunes of all time!

VOLUME 1

00240221	C Edition	$39.99
00240224	Bb Edition	$39.99
00240225	Eb Edition	$39.99
00240226	Bass Clef Edition	$39.99
00240292	C Edition 6 x 9	$35.00
00240339	Bb Edition 6 x 9	$35.00
00147792	Bass Clef Edition 6 x 9	$35.00
00451087	C Edition on CD-ROM	$29.99
00200984	Online Backing Tracks: Selections	$45.00
00110604	Book/USB Flash Drive Backing Tracks Pack	$79.99
00110599	USB Flash Drive Only	$50.00

VOLUME 2

00240222	C Edition	$39.99
00240227	Bb Edition	$39.99
00240228	Eb Edition	$39.99
00240229	Bass Clef Edition	$39.99
00240293	C Edition 6 x 9	$35.00
00125900	Bb Edition 6 x 9	$35.00
00451088	C Edition on CD-ROM	$30.99
00125900	The Real Book – Mini Edition	$35.00
00204126	Backing Tracks on USB Flash Drive	$50.00
00204131	C Edition – USB Flash Drive Pack	$79.99

VOLUME 3

00240233	C Edition	$39.99
00240284	Bb Edition	$39.99
00240285	Eb Edition	$39.99
00240286	Bass Clef Edition	$39.99
00240338	C Edition 6 x 9	$35.00
00451089	C Edition on CD-ROM	$29.99

VOLUME 4

00240296	C Edition	$39.99
00103348	Bb Edition	$39.99
00103349	Eb Edition	$39.99
00103350	Bass Clef Edition	$39.99

VOLUME 5

00240349	C Edition	$39.99
00175278	Bb Edition	$39.99
00175279	Eb Edition	$39.99

VOLUME 6

00240534	C Edition	$39.99
00223637	Eb Edition	$39.99

Also available:

00154230	The Real Bebop Book	$34.99
00240264	The Real Blues Book	$34.99
00310910	The Real Bluegrass Book	$32.50
00240440	The Trane Book	$22.99
00125426	The Real Country Book	$39.99
00240137	Miles Davis Real Book	$19.95
00240355	The Real Dixieland Book C Edition	$32.50
00122335	The Real Dixieland Book Bb Edition	$32.50
00240235	The Duke Ellington Real Book	$19.99
00240268	The Real Jazz Solos Book	$30.00
00240348	The Real Latin Book C Edition	$37.50
00127107	The Real Latin Book Bb Edition	$35.00
00120809	The Pat Metheny Real Book	$24.99
00240358	The Charlie Parker Real Book	$19.99
00118324	The Real Pop Book – Vol. 1	$35.00
00240331	The Bud Powell Real Book	$19.99
00240437	The Real R&B Book	$39.99
00240313	The Real Rock Book	$35.00
00240323	The Real Rock Book – Vol. 2	$35.00
00240359	The Real Tab Book	$32.50
00240317	The Real Worship Book	$29.99

THE REAL CHRISTMAS BOOK

00240306	C Edition	$32.50
00240345	Bb Edition	$32.50
00240346	Eb Edition	$32.50
00240347	Bass Clef Edition	$32.50
00240431	A-G CD Backing Tracks	$24.99
00240432	H-M CD Backing Tracks	$24.99
00240433	N-Y CD Backing Tracks	$24.99

THE REAL VOCAL BOOK

00240230	Volume 1 High Voice	$35.00
00240307	Volume 1 Low Voice	$35.00
00240231	Volume 2 High Voice	$35.00
00240308	Volume 2 Low Voice	$35.00
00240391	Volume 3 High Voice	$35.00
00240392	Volume 3 Low Voice	$35.00
00118318	Volume 4 High Voice	$35.00
00118319	Volume 4 Low Voice	$35.00

THE REAL BOOK – STAFF PAPER

00240327		$10.99

HOW TO PLAY FROM A REAL BOOK

00312097		$17.50

THE REAL BOOK – ENHANCED CHORDS

00151290		$29.99

Complete song lists online at www.halleonard.com

HAL•LEONARD®

Prices, content, and availability subject to change without notice.

7777 W. BLUEMOUND RD. P.O. BOX 13819 MILWAUKEE, WI 53213

0817

ALL JAZZED UP!

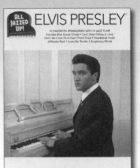

FROM HAL LEONARD

In this series, popular favorites receive unexpected fresh treatments. Uniquely reimagined and crafted for intermediate piano solo, these tunes have been All Jazzed Up!

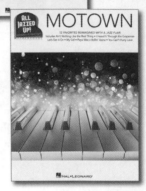

J.S. BACH
Air on the G String • Aria • Bist du bei mir (Be Thou with Me) • Gavotte • Jesu, Joy of Man's Desiring • Largo • March • Minuet in G • Musette • Sheep May Safely Graze • Siciliano • Sleepers, Awake (Wachet Auf).
00151064..$12.99

THE BEATLES
All My Loving • And I Love Her • Come Together • Eight Days a Week • Eleanor Rigby • The Fool on the Hill • Here, There and Everywhere • Lady Madonna • Lucy in the Sky with Diamonds • Michelle • While My Guitar Gently Weeps • Yesterday.
00172235..$12.99

CHRISTMAS SONGS
Blue Christmas • The Christmas Song (Chestnuts Roasting on an Open Fire) • Christmas Time Is Here • Do You Hear What I Hear • Feliz Navidad • Have Yourself a Merry Little Christmas • I'll Be Home for Christmas • Merry Christmas, Darling • Silver Bells • Sleigh Ride • White Christmas • Winter Wonderland.
00236706..$12.99

COLDPLAY
Clocks • Don't Panic • Every Teardrop Is a Waterfall • Fix You • Magic • Paradise • The Scientist • A Sky Full of Stars • Speed of Sound • Trouble • Viva La Vida • Yellow.
00149026..$12.99

DISNEY
Belle • Circle of Life • Cruella De Vil • Ev'rybody Wants to Be a Cat • It's a Small World • Let It Go • Mickey Mouse March • Once upon a Dream • Part of Your World • Supercalifragilisticexpialidocious • Under the Sea • When She Loved Me.
00151072..$12.99

JIMI HENDRIX
Castles Made of Sand • Crosstown Traffic • Fire • Foxey Lady • Hey Joe • Little Wing • Manic Depression • Purple Haze • Spanish Castle Magic • The Wind Cries Mary.
00174441..$12.99

BILLY JOEL
And So It Goes • Honesty • It's Still Rock and Roll to Me • Just the Way You Are • The Longest Time • Lullabye (Goodnight, My Angel) • My Life • New York State of Mind • Piano Man • The River of Dreams • She's Always a Woman • She's Got a Way.
00149039..$12.99

MOTOWN
Ain't Nothing like the Real Thing • How Sweet It Is (To Be Loved by You) • I Can't Help Myself (Sugar Pie, Honey Bunch) • I Heard It Through the Grapevine • I Want You Back • Let's Get It On • My Girl • Never Can Say Goodbye • Overjoyed • Papa Was a Rollin' Stone • Still • You Can't Hurry Love.
00174482..$12.99

NIRVANA
About a Girl • All Apologies • Come as You Are • Dumb • Heart Shaped Box • In Bloom • Lithium • The Man Who Sold the World • On a Plain • (New Wave) Polly • Rape Me • Smells like Teen Spirit.
00149025..$12.99

OZZY OSBOURNE
Crazy Train • Dreamer • Flying High Again • Goodbye to Romance • Iron Man • Mama, I'm Coming Home • Mr. Crowley • No More Tears • Over the Mountain • Paranoid • Perry Mason • Time After Time.
00149040..$12.99

ELVIS PRESLEY
Blue Suede Shoes • Can't Help Falling in Love • Cryin' in the Chapel • Don't • Don't Be Cruel (To a Heart That's True) • Heartbreak Hotel • I Want You, I Need You, I Love You • Jailhouse Rock • Love Me Tender • Suspicious Minds • The Wonder of You • You Don't Have to Say You Love Me.
00198895..$12.99

STEVIE WONDER
As • Ebony and Ivory • For Once in My Life • I Just Called to Say I Love You • I Wish • Isn't She Lovely • My Cherie Amour • Ribbon in the Sky • Signed, Sealed, Delivered I'm Yours • Sir Duke • Superstition • You Are the Sunshine of My Life.
00149090..$12.99

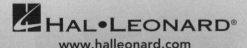

www.halleonard.com

Prices, contents and availability subject to change without notice.

Disney characters and artwork © Disney Enterprises, Inc.

0717